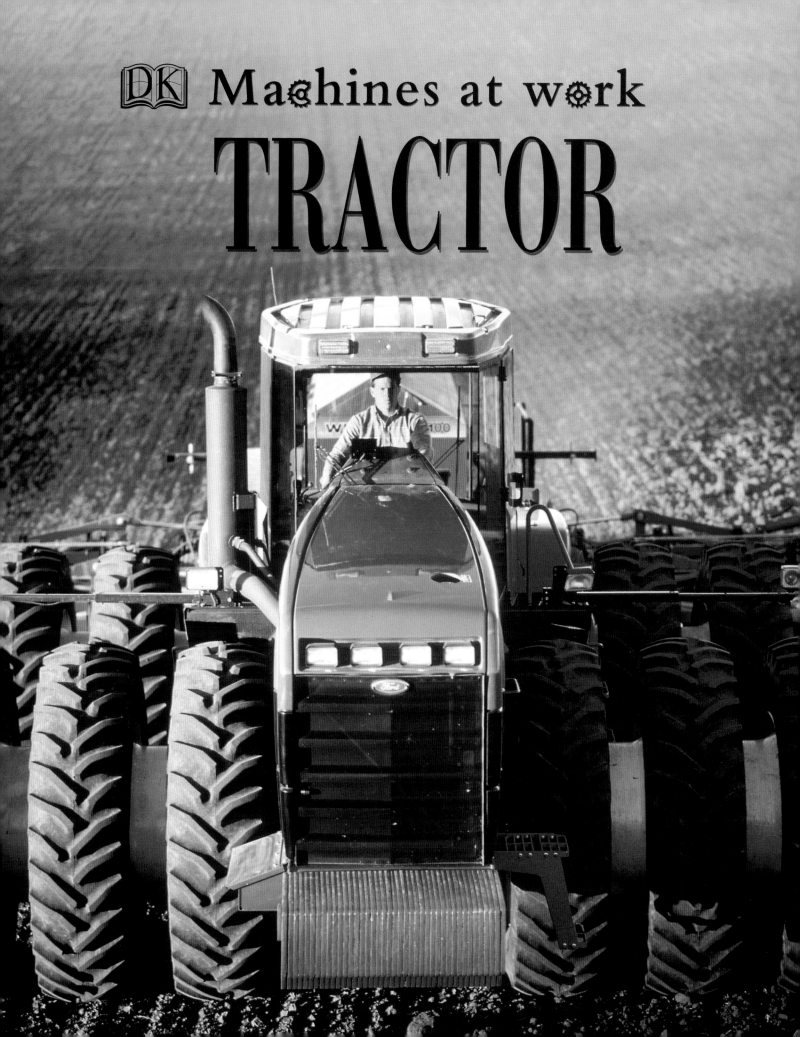

DK Machines at work
TRACTOR

LONDON, NEW YORK, MUNICH,
MELBOURNE, and DELHI

Written and edited by Caroline Bingham
Designed by Cheryl Telfer

Publishing manager Sue Leonard
Managing art editor Clare Shedden
Jacket design Bob Warner
Picture researcher Sarah Stewart-Richardson
Production Janet Leversey
DTP Designer Almudena Díaz
Consultant Michael Williams

First American Edition, 2004

Published in the United States by DK Publishing, Inc.
375 Hudson Street, New York, New York 10014

04 05 06 07 08 10 9 8 7 6 5 4 3

Copyright © 2004 Dorling Kindersley Limited

Library of Congress Cataloging-in-Publication Data

Bingham, Caroline, 1962-
  Tractor / by Caroline Bingham.-- 1st American ed.
    p. cm. -- (Machines at work)
Contents: Climb on board! -- Let's get ploughing
-- In with the seeds -- Crop care -- Harvest time
-- Going underground -- Bale it up -- Cotton harvest
-- Other farm vehicles -- It's a monster! -- Vineyard
-- Go, tractor go! -- Days of old -- Picture gallery.
  ISBN 0-7566-0217-3 (PLC)
  1. Farm tractors--juvenile literature. [1. Tractors. 2. Farm
equipment.] I. Title. II. Series: Machines at work (DK Publishing,
Inc.)
  S711.B52 2004
  631.3'72--dc22
                                    2003016050

Color reproduction by
Media Development and Printing Ltd., Great Britain.
Printed and bound in China by Toppan Printing Co., Ltd.

Discover more at
www.dk.com

Contents

Climb on board!

The **tractor** is the farmer's workhorse. This amazing machine can be hitched to all kinds of equipment to plow, lift, and carry around the farm.

It's smart, too
This tractor's onboard computer will record its movements and, with the press of a button, will repeat them as required.

A tractor has mirrors and lights, just like a truck or car.

Turn to the left

The smaller front wheels are used for steering the tractor. They can pull the tractor around in a very tight circle.

Today's tractors have a cab that protects the driver from the weather.

A counterweight helps to balance the weight at the back.

A good grip

The treads on a tractor tire are as deep as your fingers are long. These treads grip the earth— it is almost impossible for a tractor to be bogged down in mud.

Power pack

A tractor's hood hides a powerful engine. In terms of replacing the power of a horse, many farm tractors produce the work of more than 100 horses.

Let's get plowing!

After a crop has been harvested, a field is sometimes **plowed** to cut and turn the soil. The plow's blades make grooves called furrows.

What's the hitch?

Three hitches at the back of a tractor link up to the plow. They are controlled by levers in the cab.

The early bird...
The freshly turned earth is a magnet for birds, who will swoop down to pick out the worms and insects that have been exposed.

The farmer watches where to lower the plow to begin plowing.

The sharp blades will cut and turn the soil.

Pulling power

A plow is used to prepare the earth for sowing seeds. It is pulled by the tractor, and easily replaces the work of 100 people.

All ready for a new row.

At the end of a row, the plow is turned so the top blades cut into the earth.

OVLAC

In with the seeds

Once the ground has been prepared, it's time to sow the seeds. A **seed drill** can be used to sow many rows at the same time.

This seed drill has one large hopper to hold the seeds.

Fill them up
Some seed drills have a number of small hoppers to hold the seeds. The hoppers have to be filled with seeds by the farmer.

A sea of plastic

After the seeds have been sown, some farmers cover the rows with plastic sheets to warm the soil and hold in moisture. It helps the seeds to grow.

The seeds are sucked into these tubes and fed down to be planted.

The plastic will be removed when the seedlings appear.

Making the drop

As the tractor pulls the seed drill forward, the seeds are blown down the tubes to be individually dropped into small furrows in the ground.

In go sixty rows at once!

BATEMAN

Crop care

Many large farms **spray** their crops with special substances to help them to grow. They use **crop sprayers** to do this.

The boom folds so the machine can go on roads.

Weed kill

If weeds grow among crops, they compete for food and light. This machine is spraying an herbicide, a chemical that kills the weeds but not the crop.

A liquid herbicide is stored in the tank.

Not too much damage

The booms stretch so wide that the tractor's tracks do not damage much of the crop. No spraying takes place on a windy day, since drops of spray may cause environmental damage.

Hand-weeding means the farm does not have to use chemicals.

Spray leaves the boom at the nozzles.

No chemicals here

Not all farmers spray their crops with chemicals. Organic farms use natural methods to control weeds. These workers are hand-weeding on an organic farm.

Harvest time

It's a warm summer day with no sign of rain. It's time to **harvest** the **grain.** Bring on the combine!

The harvested grain is offloaded into a trailer.

Action stations!
A combine does two jobs. It cuts the crop and separates the grain from the stalk.

A reel cut
The header contains a reel that spins as the combine moves. This draws the stalks against a cutting knife. Inside, the crop is threshed, or beaten, to separate the grain.

Let's get the job done!

On the huge wheat plains of North America, combines work together to harvest football-field-sized widths of wheat in a couple of minutes. It's a fast but dusty job.

Buzz, whirr, chomp, chomp

The header can be over 25 ft (7 m) in length.

It's a fact

🚜 A combine will harvest an area the size of a football field in just five minutes.

🚜 In one hour a combine can harvest enough wheat to make 73,000 loaves of white bread.

Going underground

Root crops are crops that develop underground, such as **carrots** and **turnips**. It is possible to harvest these by machine.

Carrots are usually sold without their leaves.

Pull and cut

These tractors are harvesting carrots. The carrots are pulled up, their tops cut off, and they are dropped into the trailer.

The carrots travel up a conveyor belt.

Float on by

This tractor is picking rutabagas. The leaves have been cut off, and the tractor is lifting the roots. The huge "flotation" wheel protects the soil from being squashed.

With a grasp and a tug...

The machine grasps the carrots by their stems.

The harvester lifts two rows of carrots at once.

WHITE

Bale it up!

As summer ends, it's time to gather the **hay** and **straw** into **bales.** It will be used as winter animal feed and bedding.

The back of the baler lifts up.

Rubber belt

Dried by the sun
Hay cannot be made into bales while it is wet because it would rot. So a hay tedder is used to flip it over to dry in the sun. It also forms the hay into neat rows.

The bale is wrapped with twine or plastic netting and dropped out.

Let's make hay
Hay is often packed into brick-shaped bales. These are gathered up and stored. They need to be protected from bad weather.

In the old days
Before the invention of baling machines, hay collection took days of hard work by many people.

This baler can make 40 or 50 big, round bales of straw in one hour.

The baler is pulled by a tractor.

640 NEW HOLLAND
BALE COMMAND

K790 JYC

Rolling a bale
Straw enters the baler as the tractor drives over the dry stalks. Once inside, rubber belts roll the straw into a bale.

17

Cotton picking

Are you wearing a T-shirt or a pair of shorts? They are probably made of cotton. Cotton is picked from a **plant** by a huge **harvesting** machine.

Cotton boll

Collecting the bolls

As the cotton is picked, it fills a container behind the harvester. When this is full, the cotton is dumped into a trailer called a module builder.

Guides are lined up with the rows of cotton.

Awaiting collection

The module builder squeezes the cotton into huge blocks called modules, which are then protected from the weather.

The cotton bolls are blown into a huge container.

Guiding it in

This machine harvests four rows of cotton at once. The cotton plants are drawn in by guides. Spinning metal spikes then strip off the cotton bolls.

Each cotton plant can produce up to 75 bolls.

Other farm vehicles

Tractors are not the only machines that can be spotted on a **farm**.

You may have seen one or all of these.

Forging ahead
A Land Rover is a useful workhorse on a farm. It can even cross a flooded stream to get to work.

Time for food
An all-terrain vehicle or ATV is a fairly easy way of taking food to the sheep. There's even room for the sheepdog. And the ATV won't get stuck in mud.

Load it up

Many farmers use manure to fertilize their crops. The manure is produced by animals and is stored in huge piles. A powerful loader can quickly move a big pile.

The manure is loaded onto a truck.

The ATV is pulling a trailer.

The sheep follow the ATV because it brings food.

It's a monster!

They have the **power** of at least **375 horses** and are eight times the weight of ordinary tractors. These are the monsters of the tractor world.

This big beast

Big and strong

There is only one tractor like this. Known as "Big Roy," the tractor could win a tug of war with 600 horses.

Keep on crawling

Crawler tractors have tracks instead of wheels, which some farmers find work better on their farm's soil.

has twelve wheels.

Air needed by the engine is sucked in through this big pipe.

Spread the load
Tractors as heavy as this could damage a farmer's land. The triple wheels help to spread the weight over a larger area.

CASE INTERNATIONAL

Vineyard

Millions of **grapes** are harvested every year to make juice and wine. Some are picked by hand, but large vineyards often use mechanical harvesters.

Narrow lanes

Grape harvesters are often built to straddle a row of vines, but tractors used in vineyards have to be slim enough to drive between the rows.

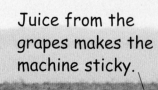

Juice from the grapes makes the machine sticky.

The grapes are shaken off the vine by the action of these strips.

Shake and drop

A tractor called a harvester is used to pick the grapes. This gently shakes the vines, causing the grapes to fall onto a conveyor belt that carries them to a bin.

On the way

Once the bin is full, the grapes are emptied into a truck and taken to be weighed. These grapes will be used in food or juice.

Go, tractor, go!

A huge **tractor** roars into life, the weight it is hauling forcing its front **tires** off the ground. The excited crowd cheers. Enter the thrilling world of **tractor pulling**.

Going the distance
Each of the tractors in the competition aims to pull a weighted sled as far along a marked track as it can.

The power and weight pulls up the front wheels.

Noise fills the air.

A starter light has given the driver the all-clear.

The farther forward the referee moves the weight, the harder it is to pull the sled.

A heavy weight
Sometimes a referee sits in a control cab on top of the sled. He or she moves the weight forward.

The rear wheels can spin, digging into the track.

Hopper

Days of old

From **horses**, hand-powered equipment, and **steam** to diesel-driven tractors, farming has come a long way.

This hand-pushed seed drill was used in the 1800s. Seed in the hopper fell to the ground.

The horses wear heavy harness.

Horse power
Animals have been used by farmers for thousands of years. Heavy horses were used very widely from the 1700s, pulling early plows, harrows, and seed drills.

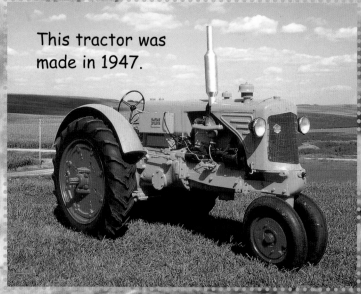

This tractor was made in 1947.

Gasoline power
Smaller, gasoline-powered tractors appeared in the 1920s. Diesel engines took over in the 1950s.

Steam power

This engine burns coal to heat water and produce steam. Steam engines were first used on farms more than 200 years ago, but they were heavy—and hungry—beasts.

Chains are used to hitch the harrow to the horses.

It's a fact

A big tractor can do as much work in a day as 200 horses.

Early combines were pulled by as many as 32 horses!

Rubber tractor tires replaced metal wheels in the 1930s.

A harrow breaks up the soil.

Picture gallery

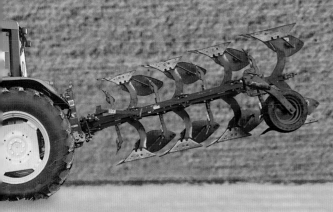

Plow

In 1837 John Deere invented a plow that did not get sticky with earth. It was a major breakthrough.

Tractor

A tractor's engine runs the tractor and powers the machinery it pulls or pushes.

Baler

Each of this machine's bales weighs the same as about 25 6-year-old children.

Vineyard tractor

Grapes are often harvested at night. It's cooler and the grapes don't break so easily.

ATV

These four-wheeled bikes are widely used on farms in Australia and New Zealand.

Combine

A large combine can hold about 17,600 lb (8,000 kg) of grain before offloading it.

Seed drill

Jethro Tull invented a seed drill in 1701 that dropped the seed in neat rows, making it easier to tend to the crops.

Tractor pulling

This sport began in the early 1900s when farmers competed to remove big boulders from their fields.

Tractor (1947)

Farmers driving early tractors were not protected from the weather, or from falls, as in the cabs of today's machines.

Monster tractor

Even this tractor's fuel tank is enormous. It holds about 20 times the amount needed to fill a family car.

Glossary

All-terrain vehicle a vehicle that can travel over all sorts of ground.

Cab the part of a vehicle that contains the driver's seat and the controls.

Conveyor belt moving rubber belt on which goods can be carried from one place to another.

Cotton boll the seed capsule of the cotton plant. The cotton is ready for picking when the bolls burst open.

Counterweight a weight that balances another weight.

Fertilizer this acts as a food for plants, helping them to grow.

Furrow a straight groove in the soil in which seeds are planted.

Harvest the process of cutting and collecting a crop.

Hitch the area where machines are attached to a tractor.

Hopper a huge container with a top that can be opened for easy filling.

Organic a naturally occurring substance that is plant or animal in origin.

Plough to turn over the soil to prepare it for planting.

Sled a vehicle that is pulled along on runners instead of wheels.

Tread the grooved surface of a tyre. Deep treads help to stop a tractor getting stuck in mud.

Index

Tracked tractor

Acknowledgements

Dorling Kindersley would like to thank:
Fleur Star for editorial assistance.

Picture credits:

The publisher would like to thank the following for their kind permission to reproduce their photographs: a=above; c=centre; b=below; l=left; r=right; t=top;

1 Corbis: Ed Bock; 2-3 Getty Images: Jean-Pierre Pieuchot; 4-5 New Holland Uk Ltd: Pharm Publicity, 5tc,c,br New Holland Uk Ltd: Pharm Publicity; 6-7 Powerstock: Javier Larrea, 6bl Getty Images: Simon Jauncey, 7t Getty Images: Fernando Bueno; 8-9 David Wootton photography, 8cl Corbis: Richard Hamilton Smith; 9tr Getty Images: Patrick Eden, 9br www.agripicture.com; 10-11, 11tr David Wootton photography, 11cr www.agripicture.com; 12-13 Getty Images: Anthony Boccaccio, 12tr Getty Images: Andy Sacks, 12c Alvey & Towers, 13tr Science Photo Library: JIM GIPE / AGSTOCK; 14-15 Corbis: George D. Lepp, 15tl www.agripicture.com, 15cr Getty Images: Kevin Horan; 16cla www.agripicture.com, 16b Alamy Images: Pictor International, 16-17 Andrew Morland, 16clb John Deere/ Pharo Communications, 17tr Getty Images: Hulton Archive; 18-19 Getty Images: Jurgen Vogt, 18tl, cr Corbis: Richard Hamilton Smith, 18cl Masterfile UK: Didier Dorval; 20-21 www.agripicture.com, 20tl Alamy Images: ANESTIS REKKA, 21tr Holt Studios International; 22-23 Andrew Morland, 22bl Case Corporation: Pharm Publicity, 22c Michael Williams; 24-25 Corbis: Bo Zaunders, 24-25t Corbis: Michael Busselle, 24tl Masterfile UK: R. Ian Lloyd, 24br Corbis: Ron Watts, 25tr Getty Images: Per Eriksson; 26-27 Jim Walbolt, 26cl Andrew Morland; 28-29 Corbis: Kit Houghton, 28bl, 29tr Andrew Morland; 30-31 Corbis: Sylvain Saustier, 30tc New Holland Uk Ltd: Pharm Publicity, 30tr Andrew Morland, 30bl Corbis: Bo Zaunders; 31tr Jim Walbolt, 31bl Andrew Morland, 31br John Deere/ Pharo Communications; 32-33 Getty Images: Guido Alberto Rossi.

All other images © Dorling Kindersley
For further information see: www.dkimages.com